Father,
Here i am
40 DAY DEVOTIONAL FOR WOMEN

JOANN ROSARIO CONDREY

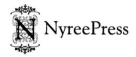 NyreePress

NyreePress books may be ordered through booksellers or by contacting:

NyreePress Publishing
A Division of NyreePress Literary Group
(972) 793-3736
www.nyreepress.com

Edited by: Robert Noland
Electronic Formatting: by Tekeme Studios
Book Cover Designed by Musikania Designs

Scripture taken from *The Message*. Copyright © 1993, 1994, 1995, 1996, 2000, 2001, 2002. Used by permission of NavPress Publishing Group./Scripture taken from the New American Standard Bible",
Copyright © 1960,1962,1963,1968,1971,1972,1973,1975,1977,1995 by The Lockman Foundation. Used by permission./Scripture taken from the Holy Bible, New International Version". Copyright © 1973, 1978, 1984 Biblica. Used by permission of Zondervan. All rights reserved./Scripture quotations taken from the Amplified' Bible, Copyright © 1954, 1958, 1962, 1964, 1965, 1987 by The Lockman Foundation

Used by permission./Scripture taken from the New King James Version. Copyright © 1982 by Thomas Nelson, Inc. Used by permission. All rights reserved./New Living Translation copyright © 1996, 2004, 2007 by Tyndale House Foundation. Used by permission of Tyndale House Publishers Inc., Carol Stream, Illinois 60188. All rights reserved./Contemporary English Version" Copyright © 1995 American Bible Society. All rights reserved.

ISBN 978-1-3019-95-981 (electronic)
ISBN 978- 0-9890039-1-9 (soft cover)

Library of Congress Control Number: 2013933632
Christian Life / Devotional

Printed in the United States of America

Table of Contents

Father, Here i am

40 DAY DEVOTIONAL FOR WOMEN

JOANN ROSARIO CONDREY

Introduction

For the next 40 days, I will be sharing with you my heart for God and for ladies just like you. My goal for this devotional is to pour out my passion for Jesus onto these pages. As we begin together, I want to share a story with you.

At the end of 2009, I found myself in a very awkward position. It seemed as if I had suddenly been moved into a desert place I had never experienced before. God had brought me out of a place where everything was comfortable, but I had not yet reached the promised land. So there I was in that "in between" place. When I finally stopped complaining, I began to realize the blessing that was there. Just like God did for the children of Israel, He began to reveal himself to me as "my God in the desert." What does this mean? I began to understand the true nature of God and realized that if I could learn to trust Him in the desert, that I could trust Him anywhere. If I could learn to hear His voice in the darkness of night, I would never be without His direction. This was a life-changing experience for me.

In this new place of revelation and communion, I began to seek God with my whole heart. In worship and prayer, I learned to make solitude, my friend, so I could spend more time with my Father. It wasn't about trying to be religious. I just began to learn how to come before Him in all of my imperfections just to say "Father, Here I Am." During one of these times of prayer, I was asking God for more. I was desiring more of His presence, more revelation of

His word....and suddenly I heard the voice of the Holy Spirit speak to me. "I can't give you more, until YOU give what you already have," he said. It's as if a light bulb came on and everything was clear. I had to find a way to sow into the lives of others everything God had been teaching me over the years. If I poured out in obedience, God would increase the anointing and revelation I was asking for. I had just had a baby at the beginning of that year and was not traveling as much as before, so I began to look for a way to obey God's instruction within the boundaries of my present season. This is how the Royal Sisterhood blog was born.

Over the years, God has honored His word. As I have poured out my relationship with God on this blog, thousands of women have been touched by God and I give HIM all the glory and praise. In return, they have blessed me with their love, encouragement and friendship. God is always faithful to His word and I see His love extended to me everyday I continue in obedience to His direction. Shortly after this, God moved upon my heart and asked me to compile some of my online devotionals into a book, which you now hold.

I pray that this is a blessing to your life. I ask that God will reveal Himself to you as you take a step toward building a relationship with Him. If you already know Him, I pray that you grow stronger in your faith and in His love. This devotional book is an outward sign of my obedience to God, and through the hard moments experienced in my "desert" I was made aware that He has a work to do through each of us. We must be in relationship with Him, so we are prepared for every moment.

For the next 40 days, I encourage you to start off your day with this devotional and your

Bible. Pray and ask God for guidance. Invite the Holy Spirit into your life and ask for your ears to be made sensitive to His voice. Ask Him to speak to you. In the quiet, listen to Him. You will be surprised how real He will become in your life.

With Love and Sincerity,
Joann Rosario Condrey

"Here's what I want you to do: Find a quiet, secluded place so you won't be tempted to role-play before God. Just be there as simply and honestly as you can manage. The focus will shift from you to God, and you will begin to sense his grace. —Matthew 6:6 MSG

Day 1

Life . . . Here Today, Gone Tomorrow

Yet you do not know what your life will be like tomorrow. You are just a vapor that appears for a little while and then vanishes away. — James 4:14 NAS

The grass withers, the flower fades, But the word of God stands forever. —Isaiah 40:8 NAS

It is so easy for us to forget that millions of people have lived before us and many will come after we are gone. We allow our lives to be controlled by fear, our own selfish desires, and so many other dysfunctions. We put off serving God 100% until "a better time," not realizing that the only time we have is NOW. Yesterday is always gone and tomorrow never comes. Why? Because it's always today!

The Scripture says that our lives are just a vapor compared to all of history. In the grand scheme of things, how does a single lifetime compare to millions of years? It just can't. . . . So what will make your life meaningful? What makes your time here well spent? How can you be certain that every day counts?

I remember my youth pastor saying, "Only what you do for Christ will last." That goal calls us to live our lives with eternity in the proper perspective. We must realize that every moment we have on this earth is precious. The only things you can take to Heaven when you die are the souls you bring to the Lord and the deeds you did in His name! (Matthew 25) You can't take any of your material things or your career with you.

So, start the next 40 days with the single goal of growing in your relationship with Jesus. Being filled with the power of the Holy Spirit, so you can impact the lives of everyone around you for Him. And when your days do finally come to an end, you can then stand before God knowing that your life counted for Him. Isn't that really what the Christian life is all about?

Heavenly Father, I ask that You would open my spiritual eyes, so I can have an eternal perspective. Help me not to focus on the temporary, so I can walk by faith and grow in my relationship with You. I commit the next 40 days to being serious about my relationship with You. In Jesus' name. Amen.

Day 2

Being Alone Isn't so Bad

After He had sent the crowds away, He went up on the mountain by Himself to pray; and when it was evening, He was there alone. —
Matthew 14:23 NAS

Many of us are afraid to be alone. We live in a society that offers constant cyber companionship and digital overload. TVs, computers, and phones are in constant use— often all at once! For those who are single, we often jump in and out of platonic and romantic relationships frequently, because we don't want to be . . . alone.

When I first got married and moved to

Atlanta, I found myself without a church and without family. At the same time, my husband worked every night until very late, so I found myself spending a lot of time alone. Living in a new city I had no one to spend time with or go out with. And there is only so much reality TV you can watch before you lose reality!

But, an interesting revelation occurred. Slowly I began to realize that this alone time was one of the best gifts I had ever received. I was allowed the opportunity to reflect on my life and to evaluate my heart. I was also able to connect with God in a very different way than ever before. This time began to train me to become more conscious of God on a regular basis throughout my day. I may not have always received an immediate answer to my questions, but our communication was continually growing.

As I have continued in this discipline of solitude, I have been able to see things about myself that are not pleasing to the Lord and He is showing me how He can change those things. At other times, I just sit in His presence and listen to a worship song. Sometimes bringing smiles of joy, sometimes tears, but each time a unique experience.

For the three years of His ministry, Jesus became both famous and infamous, constantly being pulled in every direction by his family, friends, and thousands of needy people. Everywhere He went, someone was asking for a miracle. He was constantly challenged to explain His identity, motives, or actions. In the midst of it all, Jesus was very diligent about guarding his time ALONE with His Father. He regularly stopped everything and spent hours in communion and fellowship with God. Jesus understood that the way to stay on God' s path and plan was to spend time in His presence.

I once heard someone say, "The moment you unplug your phone from the charger it begins to deplete its power." The same is true in the spiritual realm. The moment you walk out of God's presence, the world begins to deplete you.

As you go through your day, you can pray silently and let the Father know how you need His help, how much you love Him. The Holy Spirit is guiding you and hears every whisper. He will carry you when you don't have the strength to carry yourself.

So enjoy your "alone time" with the Lord. It will change your life!

Father, help me to know that even when I feel alone, You are my constant Friend and Companion. Help me to prioritize my "alone time" with You. I know You love me and long to spend time with me, and I desire the same. Thank you for Your presence in my life. Amen.

Let It Go

'This is what you are to say to Joseph: I ask you to forgive your brothers the sins and the wrongs they committed in treating you so badly.' Now please forgive the sins of the servants of the God of your father." When their message came to him, Joseph wept. . . . But Joseph said to them, "Don't be afraid. Am I in the place of God? You intended to harm me, but God intended it for good to accomplish what is now being done, the saving of many lives. So then, don't be afraid. I will provide for you and your children." —Genesis 50: 17, 19-21a NIV

My sister, I pray that your life is filled with freedom today—the freedom that can only come from the Holy Spirit.

We have all been mistreated by people in this life. Strangers can hurt us, but that doesn't usually hurt as badly as the offenses from those that are closest to us. Sometimes I wonder why the word tells us that ALL things work together for our good (Romans 8:28). Someday we may be strong enough to tell the people that have hurt us, "thank you." You may be thinking, "thank you!!! For what?!" As we look at Joseph's circumstances, we must also look at our own to see if God is trying to bring us to our destiny in a similar way.

The beautiful thing is that Joseph only expressed love, joy, and forgiveness in seeing his brothers again. That is something ONLY God can do!

Is there someone you need to let go of today? Release those offenses and forgive them by God's grace. If it seems just too hard to do, ask the Holy Spirit to begin to heal your heart and help you to let them go. There is an old adage that goes, "Bitterness is like drinking poison, expecting the other person to die." Life is too short to be bitter and bitterness will make it even shorter! Live long and live free in Christ.

Prayer

Father, I pray in the name of Jesus, that You will help me release and forgive those who have hurt me. Even if I have the right to be angry, I choose to forgive them. Holy Spirit, purify my heart and heal me, so I can truly be free to walk in Your love.

New Beginnings

Or don't you know that all of us who were baptized into Christ Jesus were baptized into his death? We were therefore buried with him through baptism into death in order that, just as Christ was raised from the dead through the glory of the Father, we too may live a new life. If we have been united with him in a death like his, we will certainly also be united with him in a resurrection like his. —Romans 6:3-5 NIV

John 10:10 tells us that the enemy comes to kill, steal, and destroy. His goal is destruction, but only as much as we allow him to. Think about this: in the things that the enemy *cannot* kill, steal, and destroy, he will begin to play tricks with your mind. He will paint pictures of relationships and situations that portray them in the most negative way possible. These "visions" will have you so worked up and frustrated that you will start the destruction yourself, because you have begun to believe in the way the enemy has painted the perception. Always remember—your mind is the enemy's battlefield. He aims much of his weapons toward your mind and spirit.

In John 10, Jesus also says that He came that we might have life and have it more abundantly. There is provision made for us in Christ to win this battle and truly live an overcoming life in Him. That's one of the reasons that I find praying in the Spirit to be a powerful resource. When I don't have the words to express to God what is wrong, then I know that the Spirit can pray on my behalf.

These moments of battle can make you feel like you are being crucified. The powerful truth is that, after every crucifixion, there is ALWAYS a resurrection when you are IN CHRIST.

This is what allows us to have a new start —no matter the defeat! Life tries to crucify us, but in Christ we can rise up and have a new beginning. No matter how dark your situation may be, you CAN have a new beginning in Christ. I pray you allow this truth to go deep into your spirit and encourage you.

You are my sister and I love you. I pray you are strengthened. Rise up in the power of His might and walk in the new life Jesus has given you.

Prayer

Father, I place my life in your hands today. I ask that you crucify everything in me that is not pleasing to you, so that I can resurrect in power, just like Jesus. Today is a new day, and I will reign with Christ, through the power of the Holy Spirit. Amen

Day 5

Word Power

Death and life are in the power of the tongue, and they who indulge in it shall eat the fruit of it [for death or life]. —*Proverbs 18:21 AMP*

Your tongue is a powerful tool. It can be used to build or tear down. It can be used to encourage or discourage. James 3 states it is a very small member, but controls the entire body. Think about your relationships. As long as positive words are being spoken, in truth and action, the relationship tends to be healthy. The same principle applies in the opposite direction. Words can destroy a relationship in the same way that they can destroy our lives.

So, as difficult as this is to face, is it time

to take a tongue inventory? Are you known for speaking positive or negative words? Building up or tearing down? Grace or gossip?

Take a few minutes in prayer and then write down what you want to change about your words. Make your list and then commit to speak life to others. Proverbs 18:21 encourages us that God gives the ability for us to change our lives, according to what we speak.

Let's take it a step further . . . let's ask the Holy Spirit what HE wants to change in our lives. Then, let's speak what He speaks concerning our lives and our situations. I know that this will yield even GREATER fruit that we can eat from.

For myself, I refuse to walk in circles, going nowhere anymore and I desire to use the keys given by God for victorious living.

Prayer

Father, Your word says that I have the power of life and death in what I confess. Teach me to be more conscious of the things I say. I will confess the positive things I want to see lived out in my life and I believe that my circumstances will eventually line up with my confession. In Jesus Name, Amen.

Never Ashamed

Thus says the Lord God: Behold, I will lift up My hand to the Gentile nations and set up My standard and raise high My signal banner to the peoples; and they will bring your sons in the bosom of their garments, and your daughters will be carried upon their shoulders. And kings shall be your foster fathers and guardians, and their queens your nursing mothers. They shall bow down to you with their faces to the earth and lick up the dust of your feet; and you shall know [with an acquaintance and understanding based on and grounded in personal experience] that I am the Lord; for they shall not be put to shame who wait for, look for, hope for, and expect Me. —Isaiah 49: 22-23 AMP

One day during my prayer and worship time, I was in our front sitting room. I had Israel Houghton's song, "Hosanna (Be Lifted Higher)" playing in the background. The sweet presence of God filled the room. My prayers quickly became exaltation to God. All I could see was His majesty! Our Heavenly Father is worthy of all glory, honor, and power. There is no one stronger or greater than Him. There is no one more loving than Him, because He IS Love. He is Mercy and Grace.

He is so wonderful and, in all honesty, He owes us nothing. We are not worthy of His love and grace, but He still extends it to us through his Son, Jesus. Father, I thank you for loving us even when we are unlovable.

He is the God of "exceedingly abundantly" and He always desires to bless us and increase us. AMAZING! This truly is a work of the grace of God. His Spirit took me to the Isaiah passage above and reminded me once again of this powerful promise.

Please take some time to study the entire chapter, if you can. Even when we have lost everything, because of our own foolishness, God makes a way to restore all that is lost. He actually will always restore MORE than what was lost, when we allow Him to have His way.

So you may ask, "What do I have to do to access this restoration in my life?" . . . Return to your God. Love Him with all your heart, soul, and strength. Put no other gods before Him. Neither your career, nor your possessions, should come between you and the Living God. Then all that you have lost will be brought back to you. As you wait on Him, remember His promise—WE WILL NOT BE ASHAMED. Expect God to do amazing things in your life, as you love Him completely.

Prayer

Lord, Your Word is true and I choose to believe it over my own experience. I will return to You, because of my love for you. I am so thankful for your mercy and grace. You are awesome. I will seek you and wait on you knowing that I will never be ashamed. You are true to Your Word and I thank You. Amen

Willing and Obedient

If ye be willing and obedient, ye shall eat the good of the land: but if ye refuse and rebel, ye shall be devoured with the sword; for the mouth of Jehovah hath spoken it. —Isaiah 1:19-20 ASV

Ladies, even though we have not always done the right thing, God is faithful to restore. God's word is definitely a word of grace, but also a word of responsibility.

A few months ago I was preaching in New York and I made reference to a song that says, "This is a season of grace." The truth is, every season can and should be a season of grace, mercy, blessing, and anything else that God has for us. When we are connected to the vine and we abide in Jesus, He will rain on us. Even when things are not perfect, His peace has a way of filling our heart and mind.

So this is where the balance comes in. If we are willing and obedient, we will be blessed. In our time of communion, we are being led in the direction He has for our lives. It may be something small or something big, but in our obedience, great blessings will come. When we are disobedient, the enemy has the opportunity to come in with condemnation, but that is the moment we should RUN to our Heavenly Father and repent. This allows the blood of Jesus to cover us and bring us back into grace.

Be willing and obedient. Hear the voice of the Lord and follow His lead. By your obedience, the windows of Heaven will be opened in your life. Don't let fear stop you from doing the things God is asking. He is with you! Just surrender and obey. You will see the blessings of God begin to manifest in your life.

What are the things God is asking of you? Are there habits that need to change? Maybe He is asking you to STOP doing something that does not please him. Your disobedience stops Him when all He wants to do is bless you. Maybe He is asking you to START something for Him. Be willing and obedient and I will rejoice with you in every blessing!

Prayer

Father, I have seen the consequence of my disobedience so many times and I ask for forgiveness. Give me a willing heart and an obedient spirit, so I can follow Your direction for my life. I know this will bring blessing and favor to me. In Jesus' Name. Amen.

Day 8

All Things Work Together

And we know that all things work together for good to those who love God, to those who are the called according to His purpose. —*Romans 8:28 NKJV*

As a minister, I try my best to be transparent because I believe that this allows for people to truly be encouraged. It makes no sense for us to pretend that we are perfect, even though we always strive for holiness, because we love God and respect His calling upon our lives.

My husband, Cory, and I fell head over heels for each other and got married in December 2008. Considering the fact that I got married at 34, I didn't want to wait to have a child. The "pill" was giving me very bad headaches, so we decided to let nature take its course. We got pregnant in February of 2009, but 8 weeks into the pregnancy we lost the baby.

Now, I understand that miscarriages are very common. My mother had two before I was born and almost lost me. But I have to tell you that from the moment we found out we were pregnant, I constantly prayed asking God not to allow a miscarriage. I will never forget when the doctor came into the emergency room and said, "I am sorry, but there is no heartbeat." "What do you mean no heart beat? I just had my eight-week ultrasound a few days ago and everything was fine!" I didn't say these things out loud, but the words were screaming inside my head. I tried so hard to keep it together and to be strong, but through the plastered smile on my face, the tears finally overtook me.

My heart broke that night, like never before. I couldn't understand why God did not honor the one prayer I had prayed for our unborn child. I would be lying if I told you that I just shook it off, but I will say that I had to find a way to worship God regardless of what had happened. I remember calling my mother and she would just pray for me in the Spirit and minister to me. I know that my entire church family in Chicago was praying for me, because I could feel the strength of their prayers. Obviously, God knew something that I didn't know and He allowed the best outcome to occur.

A short time later, Cory was out of town and sent me a text message. He referenced our miscarriage and how he felt that I had been strong during that time.

My response to Cory's text message was this: "That's something you look back on and know God carried you through it. Life is not always perfect, but God is perfect. His love for us is perfect and, in the end, He causes all things to work together for our good."

Look back over your life and remember the times that God has carried you through. This should give you faith to know that when you walk with Him, He will ALWAYS pick you up, even when you don't have the strength to keep going. It's like the old poem goes: "The times when you have seen only one set of footprints is when I carried you."

Father, I trust You with my life. I believe with all my heart that You love me and care for me. You are in control and everything that happens in my life is working for my good, even when I can't see it. Allow me to abide in Your peace.

New Mirror ~ New Image

For I am not ashamed of the Gospel (good news) of Christ, for it is God's power working unto salvation [for deliverance from eternal death] to everyone who believes with a personal trust and a confident surrender and firm reliance, to the Jew first and also to the Greek, For in the Gospel a righteousness which God ascribes is revealed, both springing from faith and leading to faith [disclosed through the way of faith that arouses to more faith]. As it is written, The man who through faith is just and upright shall live and shall live by faith. — Romans 1:16-17 AMP

Faith in Jesus is the cornerstone of Christianity. The foundation of our faith comes from believing that Jesus:

✧ is the son of God.

✧ was born of a virgin.

✧ knew no sin.

❖ died in our place.

❖ rose from the dead.

❖ will return for us one day.

To someone that has no faith, all this seems impossible. For Christians, we believe that all of the above is true and there is no way to get to God, except through Jesus. By faith, we receive the sacrifice of Jesus and we are made "the righteousness of God in CHRIST."

In the New King James Bible, verse 17 says: "For in it the righteousness of God is revealed from faith to faith." In what? What is "it?" Well, it refers to the Gospel of Christ and the salvation talked about in verse 16. The righteousness of God is revealed in and through the faith that brought you to salvation. Your faith is founded on Who Jesus is and what He did FOR YOU. He died for you! In your place, so you wouldn't have to! Everything Jesus did and everything He suffered was for you. In HIM you are a new creation. In HIM you have power. In HIM you can overcome every obstacle.

Your faith in Christ is the foundation and the seed that allows your faith to grow and become stronger. Once you really understand and believe who you are IN CHRIST, you can believe that He will be everything else you need and this causes your faith in HIM to grow. Your faith grows in believing what Jesus will continue to do FOR you, IN you, and THROUGH you.

I keep stressing the IN HIM, because we can never think that we can do anything in our own strength.

So do me a favor . . . break the mirror of low self-esteem, pride, and arrogance, and look at yourself in a new mirror—the reflection of Christ. When you look in this mirror, I pray you begin to see who you are IN HIM. This will give you a new image and allow you to see yourself differently, to live and act differently.

I hope this will inspire you to look in your new mirror and study God's word for yourself, so this new image can be revealed to you.

Father, I give You my heart. I pray, in the name of Jesus, that Your Word would be sown into it and bear fruit. Allow faith to grow in me, so I can see who I am in Christ and that the old image I have of myself would be destroyed, so I can enjoy this new image. Amen.

Day 10

Break Through

. . . for in Him we live and move and have our being, as also some of your own poets have said, 'For we are also His offspring.' —Acts 17:28 NKJV

My Sisters, I truly feel we have been receiving what the Spirit of God has been giving. As women, self-image is something that we continually struggle with. I pray right now, in Jesus name, that as we read and pray, the Word of God will break every bondage. Not just broken, but destroyed. I rebuke every spirit that tells you that God can't use you. It's a lie from the pit of Hell! The truth is: God can and will use you!

On one of my Donna Richardson Joyner exercise DVDs, she says, "What would you do if you knew you could not fail?" I had to ask myself that question and really take a look at my life.

So, what about you? How long are you going to wait before you start walking in your faith identity? How long before you allow your life to be used as God's instrument? You are God's child. The image of God is in you. The power of God is in you.

Join me in this prayer: "Lord, thank You for making me one with You through Jesus. Now, teach me how to access everything that You are. In my life I want to MANIFEST Your power, patience, love, grace, mercy, and humility. I desire to be a reflection of who You are."

This is the way we will be able to draw lost souls into the Kingdom of God. When people see that we are different, they will be impacted by our lives. This will make them more open when we share our faith or invite them to church, because they will see something in us that is REAL.

Be blessed today and walk in your royalty. Spend time with your Heavenly Father and allow Him to download His image into you. I promise you will begin to see a change that will make both you and your Heavenly Father smile.

Prayer

Father, I am Your child because You purchased my life through Your Son's sacrifice. Break every hindrance in me that won't allow me to walk in my true identity. Bring me into a deeper relationship with You, so I can be filled with Your thoughts. This will help me to see myself through Your eyes.

Day 11

Hear My Voice

Then I heard the voice of the Lord saying, "Whom shall I send? And who will go for us?" And I said, "Here am I. Send me!" —Isaiah 6:8 NIV

Here I am! I stand at the door and knock. If anyone hears my voice and opens the door, I will come in and eat with them, and they with me. —Revelation 3:20 TNIV

There are moments in life when you aren't expecting a move of God, because it's not "Sunday Morning." But God can move upon us very unexpectedly. For example, I am often surrounded by God's presence as I write.

I recently had a friend come over to help me with office work. As we toiled and talked, God kept weaving His way in and out of the conversation. It was such an amazing experience.

The Father allowed us to share and fellowship as sisters, but He would interject whenever He had something to say to either of us.

My husband, Cory, always says that you need to have the right person across from you for certain things to come out of you. What I love the most is that during the conversation, I could hear God's voice speaking to me through this young lady. So much heavenly wisdom was being poured out on my friend and I. It was refreshing, feeling His presence. From her reaction at different times during the evening, I believe she heard God also.

Right now, there are radio waves all around you, but you can't hear them. Why? Because you don't have a receiver. The moment you turn on a radio, you are able to pick up all those signals and hear the broadcast. I believe God is always speaking, but I also believe that we are not always in the position to hear Him. Know this—you do not have to live a moment of your life disconnected from God.

I hear God speak to me through many different methods. I hear His voice through the Word of God. Other times I hear his voice when I pray. He speaks through pastors, and even sometimes, through a homeless person on the street who may never speak a word. Before I became pregnant with our daughter, my 4-year-old niece told me that I was going to have a girl. I asked her how she knew and she said God had told her. Well, sure enough, that girl she was talking about was born February 24, 2010, our daughter Arianna.

I pray that your spiritual ears will tune in to God's voice. I pray that you can hear Him more clearly than all the noise and distractions. If you can hear his voice, you will then know what to do. There is no fear, because we will know exactly what His will is for every decision we must make. Who will I marry? Is the business opportunity I'm considering really your will? God knows the answer to every question we have.

One of the most frequent questions asked by believers is, "How do I hear God's voice?" You begin by being honest with Him. The Word tells us that the Holy Spirit will teach us all things (John 14:26). So it's okay to say, "Father, I want to hear Your voice, so I can obey Your will. So I ask that the Holy Spirit will teach me to hear Your voice."

God resists the proud, but He gives grace to the humble (James 4:6). Humble yourself before him and He will reveal Himself to you and teach you what you don't know.

God is speaking. Simply quiet your heart and listen.

Prayer

Lord, I love You with all my heart and I want to please You! Tune my ears to Your voice. Show me the path that You have planned for my life. Give me direction, so I can honor You everyday. I know You are speaking to me, so I ask that You teach me to hear You by the power of the Holy Spirit. Amen

Priceless Treasure

. . . the mystery that has been kept hidden for ages and generations, but is now disclosed to the Lord's people. To them God has chosen to make known among the Gentiles the glorious riches of this mystery, which is Christ in you, the hope of glory. We proclaim him, admonishing and teaching everyone with all wisdom, so that we may present everyone fully mature in Christ. —Colossians 1:26-28 TNIV

I have heard so many sermons on this passage my entire life. It's really amazing how we can become desensitized when we hear something over and over again. This is the reason why a new believer will take off running with their revelation, while the classic Christian will warm the pew and not much else.

Our faith cannot be compared to any

other religion in the world. Our Savior gave His very life in our place, in order to redeem and rescue us. His sacrifice and resurrection purchased a way for us to escape this meaningless existence and become one with our Creator.

Recently, I received a call from a friend of mine. Her son had had a seizure and she asked me to pray. I immediately began to pray with her and asked God to intervene in the situation. I believed that her son was made whole. While praying, my mind came back to the verse above. Christ is IN ME. This made me pray with a different confidence. In Matthew 17:14-18, we see where a man came to Jesus asking for healing for his son. The boy was having seizures and the disciples could not heal him. It seemed that the disciples didn't have enough faith to cast out the spirit of infirmity, according to Jesus. Jesus rebuked the spirit and IMMEDIATELY the boy was healed.

I pray that the Holy Spirit will reveal Jesus

to you in such a real way that you can walk in the same power.

Christ LIVES in His followers. The Jesus that conquered death is alive and His life can be manifested through ours. No other religion in the world can claim this type of power on earth. Believers that are truly able to become one with this revelation are those that (in my opinion) are used in healing the sick. They literally become Jesus on earth.

The treasure in you is priceless. Walk in that reality as the Holy Spirit reveals the mysteries of God to you.

Prayer

Holy Spirit, You were sent to us to reveal Jesus in all His power and glory. We desire to know Him and become one with Him. Christ is in us and we want to be His exact image on the earth. Take our lives and remove everything that is not pleasing to You, so we can release the power of Christ in us.

Day 13

Stop the Grumbling

Now the people complained about their hardships in the hearing of the LORD, and when he heard them his anger was aroused. Then fire from the LORD burned among them and consumed some of the outskirts of the camp. —Numbers 11:1 NIV

When things are changing all around me, I can know that it is all for my good, but it is still uncomfortable. I am the type of person that gets accustomed to things being a certain way. I find comfort in the routine. There is only one problem with this—promotion requires change. Every time I find myself kicking and screaming because I am uncomfortable, God is usually bringing the change. And I repeat—this transition is always for my good, even if it doesn't feel that way.

When sudden changes make me feel frustrated and uncomfortable, and I begin to dwell on that emotion, I can come extremely close to complaining. I try to quickly think about the children of Israel. While in the desert, they constantly grumbled about their circumstances. No miracle could keep them content for very long. They didn't understand that their discomfort was just part of the journey to the Promised Land.

Be very careful as you travel your journey. The attitude of thanksgiving and praise will get you to the Promised Land faster than the complaining route. Prayerfully, we can soon arrive at a moment where we truly understand that God is in control. Every hardship and every victory plays a part in forming our character. This formation prepares us for the Promised Land that lies before us.

Keep praise on your lips, my Sisters.

Lord, I understand that challenges come in life and they are never easy. Teach me to trust You. Guard my lips from complaining and help me to praise You at all times.

Day 14

Guard Your Heart

Keep your heart with all diligence, For out of it spring the issues of life. —Proverbs 4:23 NKJV

Let's be thankful for a new day and a new start. It's like seeing that first sign of new leaves on trees after a long winter. God has given us so many tools to help us every day. He has given us the blood of Jesus to wash away all sin. God has also blessed us with the presence of the Holy Spirit to walk with us and guide us into all truth. Let us not forget that which can be a blessing or a curse to us all—the free will that He gave each of us.

It was never our Father's intention for His

children to be robots, because He wanted us to love Him freely, by choice. Free will plays a big part in our daily lives and in the outcomes we see. This brings me to my thought for today, which was inspired by the Father.

Guard your heart with all diligence for it is very precious and needs protection. Now, I am not saying that you should build a military fort around your heart and not let anyone in. To love others, you must be open to people who have shown themselves to be trustworthy. At the same time, realize that even the people closest to you will not always fulfill your expectation. You have very close friends that might choose to betray you sooner than you think.

We cannot control what people do, but we CAN choose how we will react to them. Guard your heart and keep bitterness away. Choose to forgive, and even love your enemies, as Jesus told us to do. That doesn't mean that you have to remain best friends with someone who is obviously out to hurt you. You can remove that person from your life, but still release them, forgive them, and love them. Never wish ill against them or speak badly about them. Let them go and allow God to be the Judge of their actions.

This will keep you in the "blessing zone," because there will be no hindrance to stop the blessing of God in your life. The Word of God even tells us that if we know a brother or sister has an issue against us, leave our offering at the altar and go make it right (Matthew 5:23-24).

A loving and forgiving heart is a healthy heart. It will bring long life to you. And that's what we all want!

Prayer

Lord, my heart has been hurt many times and I have had the right to be angry, but at this moment I choose to release my pain to You. I forgive those that have hurt me and I bless them. Heal my heart and make it whole, so I can walk in love and forgiveness every day, by Your grace.

Obedience is Better

And Samuel said, Has the Lord as much delight in offerings and burned offerings as in the doing of his orders? Truly, to do his pleasure is better than to make offerings, and to give ear to him than the fat of sheep. —1 Samuel 15:22

It's interesting to me that when God wants me to notice something, He will speak the same message through different methods. The things He is revealing are the missing links that will bring those changes. With all my heart I believe through His voice, we can truly have breakthrough and change in our lives like never before.

Our obedience to God is more pleasing to Him than anything. Sometimes we would rather make a sacrifice than just obey what God says. When we do this, it is like saying to Him, "Lord, I am smarter than You and my plan is better!" Nothing could be farther from the truth. We get uncomfortable when God's instruction does not match what we WANT to do. It's all worked out in our "5-year plan" and God says "burn your plan and follow Me." Those words are enough to make anyone nervous . . . until we get to know Him.

God does not lie. He has never cheated and is never wrong. His track record is 100% success! You may know this already, but we seem to forget that fact when it comes time to obey. It gets even harder when you have to trust someone else who hears from God and it involves us! Like, "God told me we should sell everything we have and move to Africa!"

Your step of obedience may not be as drastic as the example I just gave. Regardless of how big or small the instruction given, it's the obedience that pleases God.

Let us have an ear to hear what God is saying. I also pray that He will give us the grace to obey Him without question. This obedient lifestyle will bring immeasurable blessings!

Prayer

Father, I am honored to have Your love and care around me at every moment. Help me to hear Your voice and give me the courage to obey without hesitation. I know You are walking with me, so there is no need to fear. I love you.

Day 16

Give Thanks

But as for me, afflicted and in pain—may your salvation, God, protect me. I will praise God's name in song and glorify him with thanksgiving. This will please the LORD more than an ox, more than a bull with its horns and hooves. —Psalm 69:29-31 TNIV

God's Word reminds us time and time again to give thanks! The writer of this text was afflicted and in pain, but in the midst of that, he took time to thank God and praise Him. This is pleasing to the Lord. As women, we carry so much of the family load, especially single mothers who must work full-time *and* take care of everything at home too. I also know there are some ladies that feel like single mothers, because even though the husband is in the home, he does not contribute anything! To all of you, I pray that God will give you more strength than ever before! You keep fighting and moving forward for the love of your children. My heart goes out to you— sincerely.

These circumstances, along with many others, are the perfect reason to get upset and angry. Sometimes the anger is so strong you don't have the words to communicate your frustration, so you keep it all inside until one day . . . you blow up!

MY SISTER! STOP AND TAKE A DEEEEEEP BREATH!

Tell me, in the midst of all the bad circumstances, is there ONE thing you can thank God for? . . . Okay, now that you found one, can you name two? Keep finding things to give thanks for. You may find that this discipline will bring your attitude back to a more peaceful place.

There may even be a bit of joy sneaking up on you.

Take a moment and notice—has someone done something nice for you recently? Say thank you and be grateful. God will use people, even strangers, to do things like letting you go ahead of them in the grocery line, just to remind you of His love.

Father, I thank You right now for Your love and kindness. I thank You for providing every need and I thank You for the air that I breathe right at this moment.

Let us make thanksgiving, to God and to people, a part of our daily lives.

I thank God for YOU!

Prayer

Lord, just like David, I will praise You at ALL times! I will lift my eyes and see Your goodness in the midst of even the worst moments. Your rod and staff comfort me, Your presence is like a blanket that covers me. You are worthy of all glory and I will live a life of praise and thanksgiving.

Day 17

Fall in Love Again

You have persevered and have endured hardships for my name, and have not grown weary. Yet I hold this against you: You have forsaken the love you had at first. Consider how far you have fallen! Repent and do the things you did at first. If you do not repent, I will come to you and remove your lampstand from its place. —Revelation 2:3-5 TNIV

Have you ever been in love? I know I have. When you are, every conversation you have seems to end up talking about the person you love. If you are away from each other, your heart aches. You can be on your cell phone for six hours before you know it and it barely felt like six minutes! Being in love is an intoxicating feeling.

Now fast forward 12 years, 3 kids, and 27

failed diets later! "Oh, if she would just be quiet?" "He snores so loud I can't bear to sleep in the same bed!" "You want me to do what? Oh NO, not me!"

Many of us have been in church so long we don't know how to be in love with Jesus anymore. We live life in a mechanical way, because this is just the way it has always been. We go to Bible studies and take notes, but never look at them again. The crisp pages of our untouched Bible complain as they are opened once a week . . . on Sunday morning.
Where is the passion? Where is the love?!

Father, teach us to fall in love with You again, that it would once again be a DELIGHT to pray and study your love letter to us, that this holy relationship would be vital to us once again.

Discipline has to play a major role in our spiritual lives. Spending quality time in prayer, in the Word, and in worship are the most important disciplines of all. Now, once we fall in love with our Father again, it really won't feel like a burden or hardship at all. That's real love.

Love motivates you to the point where the things you need to do, you don't mind doing at all. Actually, these moments will bring you joy and fill you with the sweet presence of the Holy Spirit. To know He is with you and guiding you, simply because you are giving Him room in your life. It's amazing!

Let's draw near to him and fall in love . . . again.

Heavenly Father, please forgive me for the love that has grown cold at times. Send the Holy Spirit to my life and reignite the flame of love and passion for Your presence. I will draw close to You and grow in this relationship everyday, because my heart desires Your presence.

Day 18

Correction = Love

Then the Lord God said, "Look, the human beings have become like us, knowing both good and evil. What if they reach out, take fruit from the tree of life, and eat it? Then they will live forever!" So the Lord God banished them from the Garden of Eden, and he sent Adam out to cultivate the ground from which he had been made. —Genesis 3:22-23 NLT

Love doesn't always look the way we expect it to. If you're a mom, think of your children and the many ways you show them love. Sometimes this love is expressed in an embrace. At other times, love is a firm correction. If you truly love your children, you will not allow them to do whatever they want to do. Why? Because it is obvious to the parent that the child doesn't always know what is good for them.

As I read today's Scripture, God's love

and mercy are so apparent to me. Others may think that Adam and Eve were banished from the garden, because God was angry at them. They would assume that God judges disobedience. God is just, but he is also LOVE.

Look at the world around us. Sin is out of control and it keeps breeding death as it grows. Shootings are an everyday occurrence. Can you imagine if mankind had eternal life in this sinful state? It would literally be Hell on earth, eternally. God was able to see this and made it impossible for man to live eternally on earth. But He gave us something better: the opportunity for redemption and eternal existence in a place far better than the Garden of Eden.

When you feel that God is closing a door or blocking a road, remember this point: His love motivates every decision He makes regarding us. In the end, God has made preparation for us and it's better than what we can even imagine.

Prayer

Father, I know that You are working in my life at every turn. Sometimes things don't work out exactly how I pray they will, but even then You are in control. Correct me and keep me on Your straight path for my life. I desire to please You and fulfill my eternal purpose.

Don't Be Surprised

Jesus, full of the Holy Spirit, returned from the Jordan and was led by the Spirit in the desert, where for forty days he was tempted by the devil. —Luke 4:1-2a NIV

As Sisters, we have been tackling some tough issues in our personal lives through these daily readings. Why? Because we are committed to personal growth and committed to getting this stinky flesh out of God's way, so He can really move in us and through us.

On this path, we are praying and spending time with God. We are becoming more intimate in this relationship and God is planting seeds in our spirit that will produce a harvest. That harvest is our destiny!

As you continue going deeper, don't be surprised at the enemy's attack. Actually you should consider it an honor that he would go out of his way to bother you. Above, we read that after Jesus was baptized by John, He was led into the wilderness by the Spirit of God. This was the Lord's first stop on his ministry journey. During that fast, he had to overcome his flesh and overcome Satan.

Jesus is so awesome that, even at His weakest moment, He was able to conquer Satan. Wow! That same power is available to us.

Let's keep our eyes open and recognize the attacks of the enemy. Become strengthened in prayer and God's Word. Ladies, we have come this far and there is **NO GOING BACK NOW!**

Prayer

Lord, even when the enemy comes in like a flood, You will raise a standard against him! You are my Hiding Place and You keep me from all harm. I will not be afraid and I will walk boldly knowing You will fight on my behalf. Thank you, Father.

Day 20

Light Bright

You are the light of the world. A city that is set on a hill cannot be hidden. Nor do they light a lamp and put it under a basket, but on a lampstand, and it gives light to all who are in the house. Let your light so shine before men, that they may see your good works and glorify your Father in heaven. —Matthew 5:14-16 NKJV

The truth is, everyone is watching us. They want to know if we believe what we say. If we walk, what we talk. Is this life a reality that can be lived out everyday or is it reserved for just Sundays?

One morning after a wonderful prayer time, I was having a great day. Worship was literally on my lips and praise was in my heart. Joy was overflowing! But in just a few hours, I had a conversation that threw me off. Suddenly, I was overwhelmed and frustrated to the point of tears. The person on the other end of the phone probably didn't even understand what was happening. My light got a little dim at that moment. Soon thereafter, I had to return to the Lord and call that person. I repented for allowing circumstances to "put a basket over my light."

Let me tell you, we are all a work in progress! But, even so, let's be mindful of our responsibility. We represent something much greater than ourselves. Each day, through prayer and relationship, we will be able to handle life with more grace.

So in the midst of your process today, represent Christ with your light and good works. If you happen to get a little "dim," just ask your Father for help and start over.

Prayer

Lord, It is my desire to represent You and Your Kingdom. Allow Your light to shine brightly through my life. Change me and make me more like Jesus, so the world can see a bright reflection of Your love.

Better Than Money

Happy (blessed, fortunate, enviable) is the man who finds skillful and godly Wisdom, and the man who gets understanding [drawing it forth from God's Word and life's experiences], For the gaining of it is better than the gaining of silver, and the profit of it better than fine gold. Skillful and godly Wisdom is more precious than rubies; and nothing you can wish for is to be compared to her. —Proverbs 3:13-15 AMP

When I was younger, I couldn't wait to finish school. The thought of being an adult and not having to go to school was so exciting to me. No more homework or report cards! But the truth is, life is a school in itself. Every day has the opportunity to teach us something new and we have never had so much access to information as we do now. If you want to know ANYTHING, all you have to do is *GOOGLE it*!

As a loving Father, God gives us advice for our spiritual growth in His Word, but He does not neglect the natural. Our ancestors were often made to feel low and uneducated, because of their circumstances. They were forced to live that way, but we have a choice. Because of men like Martin Luther King Jr. and women such as Rosa Parks, we live in a new day.

I once heard Pastor Sheryl Brady say, "The difference between a poor man and a rich man is what he knows." This proverb is emphasizing the value of wisdom. We may try to run after money and career to make ends meet, but it seems we should run after wisdom instead.

One of the definitions of wisdom states, "Knowledge of what is true or right coupled with just judgment as to action." So, wisdom is taking what you know and putting it into action.

Invest in the treasure of wisdom in your life, such as researching things that are of interest to you and growing as a person. Don't just say, "I don't know how to cook," do something about it. Look up a recipe and start cooking! Study and grow in wisdom, so you can grow financially too. The possibilities are endless! Wisdom is at your fingertips, so run and catch it! This will change your life for the better until you will become the best you can be!

Prayer

Father, there is so much to learn and I must confess sometimes I have been too scared to try something new. Please fill me with Your Spirit of wisdom and understanding. Take the limits off my mind, so I can be open to all the new things that You have in store for me. I can and will grow in my spirit, soul, and body.

Day 22

Protect Your Destiny

And when they were departed, behold, the angel of the Lord appeareth to Joseph in a dream, saying, Arise, and take the young child and his mother, and flee into Egypt, and be thou there until I bring thee word: for Herod will seek the young child to destroy him. — Matthew 2:13 KJV

Oftentimes, when I am done with my time of prayer, the Holy Spirit is so strong upon me that I am just in tears! My prayer for you is that you too come to understand that level of intimacy with Him. I pray that God will touch and change your life as He has and is changing mine. It is such a real experience that no one can ever take away from us!

An important truth for you today is to

understand that every attack of the enemy on your life comes for just one purpose—destruction. Every time you have fallen into sin is because the enemy set a trap and you were not strong enough in God's Spirit to stay away from it. But when you get truly connected to God, He opens your eyes to see every trap that Satan is trying to set, every cycle of attack he sends your way. God begins to empower you, so you don't fall into the same pitfall that you have been falling into for years! This is one of the great things about getting into intimate fellowship with God.

You also begin to see that all the enemy is after is destroying your purpose! When Herod sought to destroy the life of Jesus, it was the enemy working through him. Satan was trying to destroy the purpose of God in Jesus. He does the same thing today with God's children.

God has chosen you to fulfill a special purpose in your life. EVERY DAY the enemy comes at you to kill that purpose. Look around you and begin to see how he works. Then after you fall into that sin, (from anger to sexual sins) the enemy comes to load you down with condemnation and guilt, even though the blood of Jesus is powerful enough to forgive you and make your heart white as snow.

ENOUGH IS ENOUGH! Agree with me now—I bind the spirit of condemnation and I declare that you will grow in your relationship with God. Your eyes will be opened and you will have victory in every area of your life. You can become more like Jesus every day and sin MUST loosen its hold on you. The more you live in God's light and in His presence, the more darkness has no choice but to GO!

I believe in the work that God is doing in your life. Now you must protect your destiny!

Prayer

God, You are the Creator and You made me with a special purpose in mind. The enemy will try to destroy that purpose, but I will not fall into his traps. Keep me from all evil! Guide me in the path of Your righteousness. Build in me a character of integrity and holiness, so I can fulfill this plan that You have for me. Remove every enemy of my destiny and help me overcome—in Jesus name.

At His Word

When he had finished speaking, he said to Simon, "Put out into deep water, and let down the nets for a catch." Simon answered, "Master, we've worked hard all night and haven't caught anything. But because you say so, I will let down the nets." When they had done so, they caught such a large number of fish that their nets began to break. — Luke 5:4-6 NIV

I believe God is constantly trying to teach each of us to listen to Him. Be sure to pay attention to the messages that are being brought to you daily. Some of them you will have to refuse and rebuke, because they don't come from God, but others will cause your spirit to say, "Yes Lord, I hear You."

As you continue learning how to hear His

still, small voice in the midst of all the noise surrounding you, I pray that your faith will grow. I pray that you will be bold enough to obey the direction of the voice you hear.

Sometimes I will get angry at someone and walk away without resolving the issue. Then I will hear God's voice say, "Go back and apologize. Humble yourself." It breaks me down, but I have to do it.

Hearing the voice of God is an honor. It's a privilege. The more you hear and obey, the clearer His voice will be to you. You can be like Simon and reap a great harvest, because you took God at his word.

Let's get quiet and listen for His voice. Let's obey what we hear. Change is coming. And that's exactly how it will come.

Prayer

Father God, thank You for being a God Who speaks. I ask that You open my ears, so I can know when You are speaking. I will hold on to Your Word, because it is impossible for You to lie. At Your word, I will step out in faith and I will see miracles, because of my obedience. In Jesus' name. Amen.

Day 24

Only Dummies Refuse to Learn

I'm not trying to be offensive with that title and we can all be dummies at times, right? But here's a thought. Everything we need is available to us through God's Word and His Spirit. The Holy Spirit is referred to as the Spirit of Wisdom in Ephesians 1:17: *I keep asking that the God of our Lord Jesus Christ, the glorious Father, may give you the Spirit of wisdom and revelation, so that you may know him better. (NIV)*

Wisdom is personified in the Holy Spirit, and as we see in Ephesians, we can ask to receive the Spirit of Wisdom. Many of us suffer because of what we *don't* know, while others suffer because of what they *REFUSE* to learn.

Many marriages struggle, because the individuals in the marriage were raised a certain way that can be very different from each other. This can cause each person's perspective to be very narrow and offer no flexibility or openness to learning a NEW way. Many times, that new way is exactly what can allow both spouses to feel respected and bring unity in the marriage. Now let me be clear—I am not referring to moral issues. I am more so referring to preferences, such as who should take out the garbage. Just because you always saw your dad take out the garbage doesn't mean your husband HAS to take it out and you refuse to touch it. If you see that your husband is extremely tired after a long day at work and you had the day off, it's okay to help the brother out!

Wisdom is also willing to learn how to see life from the other person's perspective. Put yourself in his/her shoes and be open to a new way of thinking. The resolution to all the conflict may be in our ability to grasp a new perspective. If you dig your heels in the ground because you are "RIGHT," you may lose more than you gain.

Proverbs 1:5-8 NIV says this: *let the wise listen and add to their learning, and let the discerning get guidance—for understanding proverbs and parables, the sayings and riddles of the wise. The fear of the LORD is the beginning of knowledge, but fools despise wisdom and instruction.*

Wise people always seek to increase in knowledge. They understand that they don't know it all, so they seek truth and understanding. Let's ask the Spirit of Wisdom to be given to us. This will enable us to grow in all of our relationships and I believe God would be pleased to see this growth in us.

Will you commit with me to be open to wisdom?

Prayer

Father, I acknowledge that I don't know it all, but I understand that I have access to all the wisdom of the universe through You. Holy Spirit, I ask that You fill me with all wisdom and teach me the things I need to know. Open my mind to receive Your wisdom and teach me to apply it in my life.

Day 25

Don't Stress—God Has a Plan

When I was a little girl, it was always my dream to be a singer. I would watch Whitney Houston and say, "I want to do that one day!" Yes, I was the little girl, standing in front of the mirror, singing into her "hairbrush microphone." It was all I ever wanted to do! My mom would say to me, "You have to go to school. Singing is not going to pay the bills." I know she meant well and she was right—to a certain point.

As I got older, my desire for this dream intensified. Slowly but surely, at the age of 16, I started seeing God preparing a way and opening doors for me. It was so exciting! By the age of 19,

I had the opportunity to meet Fred Hammond and my first album was released when I was in my late 20s.

I had finally made it—my dream! But when it was time to record my second album, I lost my voice completely. . . "God, WHY?!" . . . I went through that trial for over a year and my voice has never been the same . . . but my life hasn't been either.

During that time, I went on a spiritual fast. I was seeking God because I needed answers. Once again, God made me face myself. He showed me how I had always hidden behind my voice, because I felt that singing defined me as a person. But God very quickly pulled the veil away from my eyes, as I heard him say, "Singing is a small part of your purpose, but it's not the whole picture." This is when I felt that calling of the evangelist come upon me. This process was painful for me, but it was a moment of growth that would be repeated many times in my life.

I will never forget the day I received a call from my record company. They called to let me know that they would be releasing me from my contract. Album sales had not met their expectations and they felt they could no longer partner with me musically. This was also the same day I was ordained as an evangelist. My life has taken some radical turns since then and I have learned some valuable lessons.

Please hear me now. You may have a plan for your life, just as I did, but God has the MASTER plan. His plan is greater than you can imagine. So as you live your life everyday, live with purpose—purpose from the Lord. There will be very hurtful and disappointing moments, but I pray that you remember my story at those times. You may feel as though life is closing the door on you, but it's only because God is allowing it. If you love God with all your heart and consistently surrender to His will, He will direct your path. I know it's hard, but don't stress . . . God has a master plan.

Father, I submit my plans to You. I can't see into the future and I don't know what is best for me, so order my steps at every moment and keep me in Your perfect will. Amen.

Are You Great?

I was talking to my mom one evening and she said something that has stuck with me, "Serving causes an explosion of power when I get to preach." Now, let me tell you more about my mother.

She is a woman of prayer. She seeks the Lord and loves God with all her heart. As a wife and mother she has always carried a lot of responsibility, like so many of us.

What I remember the most about my mother is that she has lived her life serving. As my dad traveled extensively while we were young, she was the one holding down the fort. She took great care of our family without complaint. Every recital, mom was there. Every book report, she put in long hours at the kitchen table with us. I also remember the cruel attitudes of church members that sought to divide my parent's marriage, trying to discredit her gifts and calling! She stood in prayer and by God's grace, she was not moved.

Now that all of her children are grown, I see her moving into a new season of destiny. When she gets up to minister, the Holy Spirit moves powerfully through her life. The reality is that my mother's life of service has brought blessing upon her and the greatest blessing is the visible presence of God on her.

Jesus said, *"The greatest among you will be your servant. For those who exalt themselves will be humbled, and those who humble themselves will be exalted." (Matthew 23:11-12 NIV)*

Do all things as unto the Lord and know that He sees everything. You may be a single woman taking care of your elderly parents . . . remember that you count in His kingdom. You may have a husband that doesn't appreciate how you keep the house clean and take care of the children . . . remember you count in His kingdom. Even if people overlook you and don't appreciate your service or sacrifice, know that you are laying up treasures in heaven and as you REJOICE in the Lord, He will be with you. You count in His Kingdom!

Prayer

Lord, You said that the greatest among us is the one who serves. This world makes me feel that I must be at the top to be great, but I refuse to live according to their rules. Purify my heart, so I can serve from out of my love for You, not looking for anything in return. I pray this will please Your heart and make You smile.

Day 27

It's Okay to Cry

It's exciting how you begin to hear the Holy Spirit teach you, as you grow in a relationship with Him.

One day, I was in our upstairs office and Arianna (our baby daughter) was taking her afternoon nap downstairs. While I was getting some work done, I heard her begin to cry. Immediately, I got up to give her a bottle.

As I was doing this, I heard the soft voice of the Holy Spirit saying, "It's the same way with your Father. No matter where you are, when you cry out to Him, He hears you." At that moment, I felt so loved. God is never too busy to take care of His children.

The LORD is near to all who call on him, to all who call on him in truth. He fulfills the desires of those who fear him; he hears their cry and saves them. The LORD watches over all who love him, but all the wicked he will destroy. —*Psalm 145:18-20 (NIV)*

Don't feel too grown-up to cry out to the Lord. He hears your prayer and will respond. All too often we cry out to everyone else—except for Him. Our Father has the power to change our lives and He works in mysterious ways. His plan is bigger than ours. So when your heart is heavy and you are frustrated to the point of tears, cry out to Him. Jesus always knows exactly what to do.

Father, many times I try to carry the weight of the world on my shoulders, forgetting that You are there to help me. Be my strength, oh Lord, and uphold me as I walk in Your ways.

Guard Your Temple

Or know ye not that your body is a temple of the Holy Spirit which is in you, which ye have from God? and ye are not your own. —1 Corinthians 6:19 ASV

I have heard the life stories of many women through my ministry. Some of those have broken my heart and caused me to shed tears. Countless women suffer silently, and in some instances, even the church has not learned to address them in a relevant way.

I have such compassion for those of you who weren't loved the way you deserved to be loved throughout your life. Maybe your father wasn't there and your mom just couldn't meet all your needs. My prayer is that the Holy Spirit would mend and heal the brokenness this has caused you.

Unfortunately, in the search for identity and security, too many women give their bodies away. As the old song goes: "looking for love in all the wrong places." Having no one to teach them the right path to take. By no means do I wish to shame anyone, but I pray that you will realize your true beauty and worth. That is a major prayer of mine throughout these 40 days you're investing in this book.

The search for significance plagues women both inside and outside the church. We want to judge the girls that pose for porn, but their actions are just the fruit on the tree. Their lives scream out, "Someone love me! Tell me that I'm special!" The truth is that we all need love and affirmation.

God is revealing your purpose to you day

by day. Your spirit and the Holy Spirit are housed together in you. Your body is the temple and dwelling place of the Holy Spirit. Trading your temple for temporary love or affirmation opens the door to even bigger issues. It can lead to a life filled with silent perversion that takes hold and won't let go. I read a book where the author shared about her struggles with pornography and masturbation during her marriage. Their troubled relationship led to frustration in the bedroom that opened the door to these issues.

I pray that if you are defiling your temple with sexual activity, you will realize that freedom can be yours. Ask God for help! If you really desire to be free, tell Him! The guilt can be shed. The shame can end. Ask Him to heal the root that causes you to allow these actions in your life. Pray for the strength to say "NO." If you can say no once, it will get a little easier every time you say it.

Guard your eyes and ears. Don't watch

movies or entertain conversations that will get your mind caught in unholy thoughts. Find a TRUSTWORTHY person to be your accountability partner. This person will be able to pray with you and talk you "off the ledge" in the midnight hours. (This has to be someone of the same sex who is not dealing with the same issues or has homosexual tendencies.)

Any bondage you experience may seem impossible to overcome now, but step by step, God can give you the strength to beat it! You can be whole! You can live in holiness. Just take little steps—and trust God.

So let God work his will in you. Yell a loud no to the Devil and watch him scamper. Say a quiet yes to God and he'll be there in no time. Quit dabbling in sin. Purify your inner life. Quit playing the field. Hit bottom, and cry your eyes out. The fun and games are over. Get serious, really serious. Get down on your knees before the Master; it's the only way you'll get on your feet. —James 4:7 MSG

Prayer

Lord, I present my body to You as a living sacrifice. Purify me completely and make me whole. Heal my heart, so I will only go to You for the love I need. The past is behind me and I will live in purity by the power of Your Holy Spirit. I trust You to be my Strength and make me whole.

Day 29

Stay in His Face

"There is no fear in love. But perfect love drives out fear, because fear has to do with punishment. The one who fears is not made perfect in love."—1 John 4:18 NIV

So, you have done things you are ashamed of. If we are honest, we must admit we all have. I am a strong believer in holiness and I allow no excuses for someone living in sin, but at the same time, it's my job to point people to the love of God. It is not my desire—or God's—for you to try and live holy only because you are afraid of Him, but rather, because you know it's better to live in freedom from sin.

When you understand the nature of God,

you want to honor His love for you by pleasing Him. This is why you feel bad or guilty when you fall short. This is actually a great thing! There are so many people that live in sin—all types of lustful acts—and boast proudly without shame. They are so far from God that they have become calloused to His voice of conviction.

Allow me to share with you a major key to success during the process of deliverance. Here it is: No matter how bad you mess up, KEEP GOING BACK TO GOD! The enemy will whisper in your ear and say, "God is not going to forgive you this time!" He wants to pull you away from God, because he knows that if you really get free, then you will help others find freedom also. God's presence is where we become free from sin. And it's in His presence that we STAY free from sin. All of us have to enter His presence in the same way—through the blood of Jesus.

So Joann, how do I get into God's presence, so He can change me? Honestly, it just takes time. When you meet someone that you are interested in, how does the relationship develop? Talking on the phone, going to dinner, spending time is the bottom line. For example, you are at work and it's your lunch hour. You brought your lunch to work, so you decide to eat in the car. It only took about 10 minutes to eat, so you choose to spend the rest of your hour with God. You turn on a CD to play your favorite worship song. You close your eyes and begin to sing the song to Him, meaning it from your heart. Suddenly, your spirit floods with gratitude and tears fill your eyes as you think of Jesus dying on the cross for you, because He loves you. You then simply whisper, "Jesus, I love You. I give You my life. I want to please You and I ask You to heal me, purify me, and help me to serve You." You begin to verbalize your thoughts to God. Then you may just feel like being quiet for a moment, as His presence fills your heart with His spirit.

It's not hard to develop a relationship with

God; it just takes time. Come to Him, because you know He loves you. This love causes you to no longer be afraid of rejection, because if He gave His only son for you, then He would NEVER reject you when you come to Him, especially when you are sincerely trying to get your life together.

Just stay in His face and let His light shine on you to change you.

Prayer

Father, I draw close to You, because of Your love for me. I am precious to You and this gives me joy. When I fall short, I ask You to forgive me and cleanse me with the blood of Jesus. Help me to become stronger every day, so I can look like You. Amen.

Day 30

Look For the Escape Route

No temptation has overtaken you except what is common to mankind. And God is faithful; he will not let you be tempted beyond what you can bear. But when you are tempted, he will also provide a way out so that you can endure it. —1 Corinthians 10:13 NIV

I was staring into our fireplace one night and a thought came to me. In order for the fire to keep burning, you must keep feeding the fire. Something has to be constantly burned up for the fire to be a fire!

Have you ever heard the phrase, "I want to be on fire for God"? Well, every time we put our flesh into God's refining fire, we keep that fire of holiness and consecration burning. That's when you can see what you are made of.

Fire removes the impurities from precious metals. It removes the contaminants that taint and devalue. Trials and temptations come to us all and they work as a purifying fire. We are all tried in the fire, but we can trust God's promise that He won't place more on us than we can bear. He knows what we can handle and He desires for us to become stronger by trusting in Him.

When the temptation or trial feels too heavy, remember these truths:

1—Remind yourself of God's promise to you.

Even when you walk through the valley of the shadow of death, He is with you.

2—Ask the prayer warriors in your life to pray with you and help you carry the load.

3—God's word promises that He will make a way of escape, as we see in today's verse.

4—We always have a choice to NOT sin.

Sometimes we give in so quickly that we forget to look for that way of escape. EVERY time we are tempted, there is a way out, and we must take it.

Prayer

Father, I thank You for Your faithfulness. You are aware of everything that is happening in my life at this very moment. When I feel overwhelmed, remind me to ask for Your strength right then. You know how much I can handle and I ask that in the midst of my weakness that You are glorified. I lay my burden at Your feet and thank You for Your help. Amen.

Provision in Purpose

The LORD had said to Abram, "Go from your country, your people and your father's household to the land I will show you. "I will make you into a great nation, and I will bless you; I will make your name great, and you will be a blessing. I will bless those who bless you, and whoever curses you I will curse; and all peoples on earth will be blessed through you." —Genesis 12:1-3 NIV

Provision seems to be a common struggle for many people. We look at the economy and everyone seems to be affected in one way or another. Maybe your income has dwindled or even made non-existent. There always seems to be more month than money. If everyone is suffering through this, then there must be no relief for anyone. We are all in the same boat, right? WRONG.

This devotional is not about your income or how much money you have in the bank. It's about provision in purpose. Provision is not always about money. In Genesis 12, we see how God is giving Abram *specific* instructions. God told him to leave his country, his people, his family and go. Go where? "TO THE LAND I WILL SHOW YOU . . ." In God's direction, there was a destination. It was a mystery location. Abram knew he was going somewhere, but didn't have the exact coordinates.

Sometimes you feel just like Abram. You know God has spoken, but you feel as if He only gave you half the directions. WELL, HE DID! Our Father understands human nature far better than we do. If He gave you the exact address, then you would leave right away and take the route that suits you best. There is only one problem with that. Your route will not form the character in you that you need for the destination. So, God gives you instructions that take you to the first intersection, knowing that when you get there, you will have to consult Him for further instructions. For us, it's often all about the destination, but for God it is always all about the journey.

After God tells Abram to go, He gives him an amazing promise. Now if Abram had stayed in his country, with his people, and in his father's home, would he have received this promise of blessing? The answer is no. The promise was to be released as Abram followed his purpose. If you continue to read, it's obvious to see that the promise was manifested. It's actually so strong that the Jewish people are still a very blessed and prosperous people.

If we concern ourselves more with our purpose and God's specific instruction, the provision will become evident. Even if your purpose calls for you to leave your six-figure salary to become a full-time missionary, you will never lack God's provision. Like my husband, Cory, says, "Don't chase money. Chase the vision."

Prayer

Jehovah Jireh, You are my provider. Teach me not to focus on my financial situation. I set my eyes on my purpose—Your purpose for me. You have a plan for my life and I am excited to see what You are getting ready to do.

Day 32

Saying "No" To Desperation

There are times when I am praying in the Spirit, but I can feel the spirit of discouragement trying to creep in. When that particular spirit comes, it tries to attach itself to us like a leach. It wants to suck the life and strength right out of us! This spirit tries to hang on as long as possible to stop us from "pressing toward the mark." If you don't open your spiritual eyes and begin to fight against that spirit immediately, it begins to grow.

Discouragement actually grows from feeding off your fear and other negative thoughts that you entertain because you feel "discouraged." This state makes you look around in hopelessness and causes panic to knock on your door. "What am I going to do now?!" "Has God forgotten me?!" All these questions flood your mind and push you to the next level . . . desperation.

Desperation will rob you of any peace that you had left. You start looking around frantically trying to figure out what to "do." You Google this, question that, and then call so-and-so. You do any and everything trying to find an answer. Desperation has tricked you into becoming your own god, because you are searching inside YOURSELF for the answer. You talk to everyone and forget to go to God. I thank the Lord for my sister, Melody, because every time I go to her feeling like this, she listens, but then points me back to God. THANKS, MEL!!!

Take your energy and your emotions to your prayer closet. Lay your burdens at His feet. Wait for His answer and don't wear yourself out trying to INVENT a solution when He already has the perfect one. Discouragement and desperation are not of God, so rebuke them and move back into faith, peace, and joy.

The Lord will soon be here. Don't worry about anything, but pray about everything. With thankful hearts offer up your prayers and requests to God. Then, because you belong to Christ Jesus, God will bless you with peace that no one can completely understand. And this peace will control the way you think and feel. —Philippians 4:5b-7 CEV

Father, I refuse to walk around in discouragement and desperation! You created the heavens, so you can handle everything I face from day to day. Fill my heart with Your peace —the peace that passes all understanding and give me faith to expect a miracle. Amen.

Don't Snap!

Each of us is on a journey throughout our lifetime. There is a path designated for us, and each day that we draw closer to God, that path is revealed a little more. But also the closer we draw to the holiness of God, the more aware we are of our imperfections. This is why Isaiah said, *"Woe to me! I am ruined! For I am a man of unclean lips, and I live among a people of unclean lips, and my eyes have seen the King, the LORD Almighty."* (Isaiah 6:5) He was convicted, because in comparison to God's holiness, we are all unclean. This is why we need the blood of Jesus to wash away our sin and cleanse us.

Although grace continually gives us opportunity to repent and change, it should not be taken lightly or taken for granted. 1 John 2:1 says: *My dear children, I write this to you so that you will not sin. But if anybody does sin, we have an advocate with the Father—Jesus Christ, the Righteous One.*

It is not God's desire that we live in sin and use the blood of Jesus as an "Escape Hell card." It is His desire that we draw close to Him. And in drawing close, He will begin to reveal our shortcomings to us. We then take this information into our prayer closet, asking the Holy Spirit to change us and make us more like Christ.

Anger is like a fire; it can be very destructive. Proverbs 29:22 states: *An angry person stirs up conflict, and a hot-tempered person commits many sins.*

You may be a person that experiences anger in a very passionate way. This passion causes you to react and many times this hurts the people you love the most. You may notice that as you are seeking God, or even fasting, that you seem to be even more short-fused than usual. Take a deep breath and know everything will be okay. This is simply God's way of drawing your attention to something in your character that needs to change.

Lately I have found that if I feel angry, rather than responding, I just need to go pray. This allows me the time to cool off, while also allowing the Holy Spirit to deal with my heart. If I am truly being changed by God, I cannot make excuses and say, "Well, God, he offended me, so I had the "RIGHT" to snap!" No! Even Jesus told us to love our enemies! I have found that during that prayer time, I begin to confess that I forgive the person. Sometimes I am saying it by faith, but it opens the door to an actual change of heart.

Anger does not have to have dominion over your life. I pray for you and encourage you to bring your emotions (good or bad) to God and allow Him to mold your character until it is pleasing to Him. If we are all seeking to be changed and walking out the process, I believe that as a whole, we will begin to look more like Christ than ever before.

Prayer

Heavenly Father, I am so grateful for Your love and patience. Continue to reveal the areas of my life that need to be changed by You. I yield to Your process. I know that You made me and You know what I need. Help me not to abandon Your process, even when I see things in the mirror that I don't like. Make me more like You, everyday. Amen

You Are What You Eat

So then faith cometh by hearing, and hearing by the word of God. —Romans 10:17 KJV

Have you ever thought that this familiar verse can also work in the opposite direction? If faith comes by hearing God's word, is it possible that fear comes from hearing the enemy's word?

Everyday you are trying to draw closer to God, while also fighting through sin, discouragement, frustration, and everything else the enemy throws at you. I ask that you STOP sabotaging your own efforts! You are what you "eat," especially what you consume through your eyes and ears.

If you want to build your faith, listen to lots of sermons on faith.

If you're believing God for a financial breakthrough, make sure to pay your tithes, THEN print out every verse on prosperity and confess it every day. I still remember my dad doing that and taping the verses to the walls of the house, so he would read it and confess it every time he walked by.

Stop watching movies that have sexual scenes in them. They only make it harder to live holy.

What conversations are you entertaining? Do they glorify God?

GUARD WHAT YOU HEAR AND SEE. What you consume is what you will become . . . think about it . . . you are what you eat!

Prayer

Lord, I come to You today asking for Your wisdom. Make my spirit sensitive to Your leading. Teach me to guard the anointing and favor that You have placed on my life. I desire to be so full of Your presence that it will be obvious to everyone that I am Your child. Thank You. Amen

Seek Wise Counsel

Where no wise guidance is, the people falleth; But in the multitude of counsellors there is safety. —*Proverbs 11:14 KJV*

You've likely heard the phrase, "You can't see the forest for the trees." Today's version would be, "It's all up in my face." We all know that it is hard to see the big picture, when you are in the middle of a situation. The circumstances can get so complicated that it leads to confusion. Trying to make the right decision can seem impossible. This is one of the main reasons that it's so important to have praying people in your life—your own prayer partners.

These people are trustworthy and

confidential. They love you and want the best for you. I want to encourage you to not feel like you have to walk alone. You don't! Open your mouth! **SEEK WISE COUNSEL!** You would be surprised how a simple conversation with a trustworthy friend can bring true clarity and direction.

Two are better than one, because they have a good return for their labor: If either of them falls down, one can help the other up. But pity anyone who falls and has no one to help them up. —Ecclesiastes 4:9-10 NIV

There is no need to try and be "wonder woman" and fail alone, when we can succeed together.

Prayer

Lord, I know I am a small member of the Body of Christ. Show me the people in my life who are also a part of Your body —those whom You have placed in my path to shed light and wisdom on things that I may be going through. I also pray that You would allow me to also be that trustworthy friend to someone, so I can be a blessing as well. Amen

Day 36

Purpose Packed Prayer

It's funny how many times we have heard something all of our lives, but it becomes crystal clear to us at a particular moment. I grew up in a non-denominational Pentecostal church. We believe in the gifts of the Spirit, including the gift of speaking in tongues. Although I'm sure there was an exact day that I began speaking in tongues as a prayer language, it now seems like this gift has always been a part of my life.

In Dave Roberson's book, "The Walk Of The Spirit, The Walk Of Power," he makes this statement: "There is a supernatural exchange that takes place when we pray in other tongues . . . He (the Spirit) prays the perfect plan of God into your spirit, so you not only know what you are called to do, but how to fulfill that call in the perfect timing, will and power of God."

The Holy Spirit was there when God created the plan for your life. Romans 8:27 states that the Holy Spirit intercedes (prays fervently) for us. As we pray in tongues, during our private prayer time, we are exchanging our ideas and our will for God's perfect plan and His will. The Holy Spirit searches our heart (Romans 8:26) and begins to remove everything that does not match up with God's perfect plan. Then He implants the plans of God into our spirit. Sometimes our mind will know what this plan is and sometimes it will be hidden in our hearts until God reveals it.

Praying in tongues is like having a direct connection from your spirit to God's spirit (1 Corinthians 14:2). It's a prayer language that goes beyond your intellect and prays the perfect will of

God for your life. The Word also tells us that when we pray in the Spirit (tongues), we are edified or built up (1 Corinthians 14:4).

If you have received the gift of speaking in tongues, you can activate that gift anytime you are in prayer. If you are feeling weak, take time to pray in tongues. You will notice a difference in your attitude. By faith, you open your mouth and allow that heavenly language to flow. You don't have to wait to "feel" something before you can pray in the Spirit.

If you have never spoken in tongues and desire to, begin to pray and ask Jesus to baptize you with His Spirit. Seek this gift, learn about it, pray for it, fast for it, seek it, until you receive it.

In Dave Roberson's book I quoted from earlier, he testifies that God called him into the ministry, so he quit his job. He decided that he would pray in the Spirit the same amount of hours he used to work, for God to provide for his family. For three months he prayed eight hours a day, but felt as if nothing had changed. At the end of that third month, he was invited to a mid-day Bible study where another man was preaching. During the message, he looked over at the woman sitting next to him and God revealed her hip problem to him, as if he were looking at an X-ray! He asked her if she had problems with her hip, then he asked, "arthritis?" She confirmed that was the doctor's report. He grabbed her ankles to pray for her and realized one leg was much shorter than the other and this made him nervous. But he shut his eyes tight and prayed anyway—and she was instantly healed!

Praying in the Spirit revealed Dave Roberson's ministry and God's calling on his life, along with the power of healing. There just may be something to this praying in the spirit, huh?

Lord Jesus, I thank You for the precious gift of the Holy Spirit. I ask that You would fill me more and more each day. Baptize me as You baptized Your disciples in Acts. I want to enjoy a powerful prayer language in the Spirit. This is Your gift to us and I receive it. Amen

Day 37

Joy Of Giving

While preparing for one of our monthly gatherings of the Atlanta Royal Sisterhood Chapter, I was seeking God to know His plan and direction for our meeting. Suddenly, my heart was filled with joy, knowing that I have the opportunity to share with my sisters and GIVE them whatever God wants them to have.

There is a yearly festival in India called "The Joy Of Giving Week." They take the entire week and host different organizations that are focused on giving. People that have other beliefs have even found the truth in our Biblical principles. Jesus Himself told us, "It is more blessed to give . . ."

When we give, we elevate our own spirit above our fleshly inclination to be selfish. It is God's nature in us that makes us givers. Yes, even unsaved people can show the nature of God in their actions, because they were created in God's image. Now, this does not mean they can earn salvation through their charitable works, but that's a completely different subject for another time.

As you ask God to give you a pure heart, you will become more giving and considerate of others. The joy of giving will exceed the joy of receiving, because of the purity of your heart. You won't have to tell everyone what you give; it will just be a joy that is deep in your heart.

This is even a great way to get past your own tragedy! When you look beyond your problems and focus on being a blessing to someone else, you will feel empowered! Your giving to others sends this message to the enemy, "I will not sit around and cry for myself, but while I have strength, I will bless someone else!" It's just like punching him right in the eye!

Be like God. Be a Giver. Discover the joy He feels every day He gives you life.

Prayer

Father, I am so blessed by You everyday! Please show me ways to give to those around me. Make me like You—a Giver. Teach me to give love, patience, and kindness, because this is one of the reasons we are on this earth. Thank You for one more day to be a blessing to someone else. Amen.

Maybe That Wasn't Such a Good Idea

With such nagging she prodded him day after day until he was sick to death of it. So he told her everything. "No razor has ever been used on my head," he said, "because I have been a Nazirite dedicated to God from my mother's womb. If my head were shaved, my strength would leave me, and I would become as weak as any other man." When Delilah saw that he had told her everything, she sent word to the rulers of the Philistines, "Come back once more; he has told me everything." So the rulers of the Philistines returned with the silver in their hands. After putting him to sleep on her lap, she called for someone to shave off the seven braids of his hair, and so began to subdue him. And his strength left him. —Judges 16:16-19 NIV

Most of us know the story of Samson and how his life unfolded. He just kept playing with fire and eventually got burned, badly burned.

One day the Holy Spirit began to show me how easily we are weakened. When we have walked in the faith for many years, we can begin to falsely believe that we are strong in ourselves. So we let our guard down, thinking we know how to handle the "Delilah's" in our lives.

Always stay aware of your surroundings and your inner circle. Who is close to you? What type of influence do they have over your life? Are they pushing you to flirt with things that you know God has forbidden? If your answer is yes, you must walk away from them immediately!

Today's Scripture passage says that Delilah "nagged" him until Samson gave up the secret to his strength. The enemy loves to bring things into your life that will nag you to death. Like a drop of water, they drip . . . drip . . . drip until you give in. You think you are strong enough to handle the pressure. It's just a little "drip," just a little prodding in the wrong direction.

None of us are infallible and if we allow ourselves to stay in the wrong company, our character will compromise what is right. If something or someone is pulling you down—get away. Don't wait until your head is shaved and your eyes are plucked out to say, "Hmmm, maybe that wasn't such a good idea . . . "

Lord, You have kept me to this point and I thank You. Please open my eyes to recognize those that are a bad influence in my life. Give me the strength to walk away from them. I don't want to endanger myself, because of bad company. Protect me and show me Your direction always. Amen.

Look Past The External

But the LORD said to Samuel, "Do not consider his appearance or his height, for I have rejected him. The LORD does not look at the things people look at. People look at the outward appearance, but the LORD looks at the heart." —— 1 Samuel 16:7 NIV

How many times have you looked at someone and, without knowing that person, you judged them? We have all done it in good and bad ways. We judge by what people wear or don't wear. We judge everything from hair to house. Our society has programmed us to associate certain things with success. Outward appearance is ranked **HIGH** on the list of qualities deemed important. But why are we so obsessed with the external?

As I have contemplated this question, I feel in my heart that it is just a slick trick of the enemy. Think about it. The world makes it seem that if you don't look like Kim Kardashian or Beyonce, you are not beautiful. So people become obsessed with becoming like those idols in our society. We wear what they wear and diet how they diet. We can't get up early to pray, but nothing can come between us and our morning run on the treadmill. If the enemy convinces us to be consumed with the external, he can distract us from never realizing our need for an internal rebirth.

You may be nodding your head, thinking of an unsaved co-worker at your job and saying, "Yeah, she needs Jesus!" But can I tell you this? It seems that the enemy has fed the church the same lie. Have you ever heard a spiritual person say, "I am not going to church this week, I have nothing to wear." Huh?! Are you serious?! When did your clothing have anything to do with going to the house of God? Mind you, I am not saying that we shouldn't look nice when we go places, but it should NEVER weigh so heavily that it hinders you from the true purpose of going to church. We must all be careful.

I pray that God will purify our hearts in every area. It would be a shame to look good and grand on the outside, but still be rejected by God because of our heart. Even more, it would be crazy if the person you look at and say "God can't use her" is the very ONE God raises up to lead His people in our generation. God could care less what race, color, or social status you may be. He looks at your heart.

Prayer

Father, give me Your eyes and Your heart. Teach me not to judge by outward appearance, but give me discernment to see past the external—starting with me! I know You want me to mature and this is part of that growing process. Make my heart more beautiful than my manicured hands and my pedicured feet! Give me Your eyes and Your heart, Lord.

Stop Drinking The Poison

Our world is governed by laws. These laws were set in place by God to maintain order, health, and wellbeing among His children. For example, if there were no law of gravity, we would float endlessly. So if someone steps out a window and falls, they cannot be angry at God. They knew the law. We are all aware of the law of gravity and our need for it. As a result, we cannot think ourselves more powerful than that law.

In the Spirit, there are similar laws that determine different things. We often call these Biblical or Scriptural principles. It is up to us to learn these principles, through God's word, so we can reap the blessing of living in harmony with them. For example, "give and it shall be given unto you." This verse is often quoted in many settings. It is a spiritual principle and it can work for us, if we respect and follow its instruction.

. . . but each person is tempted when they are dragged away by their own evil desire and enticed. Then, after desire has conceived, it gives birth to sin; and sin, when it is full-grown, gives birth to death. —*James 1:14-16 NIV*

Please hear me. Your quest to live a holy life affects you and everyone around you. I feel this conviction very strongly in my own heart. Ask for God's help and fight to draw closer to Him, so you can be free from every sin. James tells us that a downfall always begins with a temptation. After desire has been built up, because of the temptation, you give in to the actual sin. The sin can begin as a very small thing, but then it begins to grow and grow and grow. One sin leads to the next, until you can't even believe how far you have allowed things to go. When full grown, this sin brings spiritual death (separation from God) and in some cases it can cause physical death also.

Sin has the power to bring sickness, poverty, and many unwanted circumstances into your life—and this is not God's fault. Now, I am specifically talking about people who are DELIBERATELY living a sinful life, not individuals who are trying hard to overcome sin. The difference is in the attitude of the heart and God sees our hearts clearly.

The enemy comes to steal, kill, and destroy (John 10:10) and many times he does that by tricking us into a sinful lifestyle. But Jesus came that you might have a life free from sin—an abundant life.

Bring your sin to Him and allow Him to wash you and make you clean. Don't let your life be cut short, because you refuse to stop drinking the poison of sin. You are precious in God's sight and He has done everything in His power to reach out to you. He even went as far as sacrificing His only Son, so that you can be saved.

Please know I am praying for you.

Prayer

Father, I understand that my spirit is willing, but many times my flesh is weak. Deliver me from temptation and give me Your strength. I am drawing closer to You each day and I will not stop. Take my life and fill me with the power to overcome sin and temptation. I will live in holiness, so Your power can be made manifest in my life. Thank You for Jesus and the power of His blood. Thank You for the precious Holy Spirit, Who is always by our side. I have everything I need and I am more than an overcomer in the name of Jesus. Amen.

My sister,

I celebrate you on completing this 40 day walk with the Lord. I pray that you have felt His presence in a special way. I believe in my heart that changes have begun in your life and I am very excited for you. Please continue to set aside time with our Father everyday. It is your lifeline.

If you miss a day, don't allow the enemy to bring condemnation on you. (Romans 8:1) Our Father is always there and He is waiting to pour out His love upon you. There is no need for you to face the challenges of everyday life all alone anymore. I love you and I pray that you continue to grow in this love relationship with Jesus. It's the most precious treasure you will ever receive.

Sincerely,
Joann Rosario Condrey

About the Author

Joann Rosario Condrey is an internationally known worship leader, songwriter, author and speaker. Together with her husband, Cory Condrey, they host evangelistic crusades across the nation through The Condrey Evangelistic Association. Joann is driven by a passion to share simple principles that help people connect with their Heavenly Father. Recently, she has had the honor of being included as an author in the newly released *Sisters in Faith Devotional Bible* (Thomas Nelson, January 2013). Through her blog, *Royal Sisterhood*, she writes encouraging posts for women to grow in their faith. Visit Joann on her website at www.joannrosariocondrey.com and follow her on Twitter @joannroscondrey

To purchase copies of

Father, Here i am

in bulk, contact

NyreePress Publishing,

a Division of NyreePress Literary Group

at (972) 793-3736 or by email at

nyreepress@gmail.com

www.nyreepress.com

CPSIA information can be obtained
at www.ICGtesting.com
Printed in the USA
FFOW01n1814270415
12964FF